Shards
of a Life

By Charles Giuliano

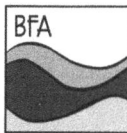

BFA

berkshirefinearts.com

Published by Berkshire Fine Arts, LLC

Book Design by Studio Two, Amanda Hill

ISBN-13: 978-0-9961715-0-2

Library of Congress Control Number: 2015936614

Dedicated to my mentor and muse Astrid Hiemer.
In memory of my parents, the Doctors
Josephine R. Flynn and Charles Giuliano,
as well as sisters Josephine and Mary-Louise.

Table of Contents

Youth 40

Music 76

Omnibus 110

Seasons 158

Introduction

Though I have written poetry off and on for decades, the works comprising *Shards of a Life* were written intensively over several months starting in the summer of 2014.

The project began with thoughts on the month of August. That led to an idea of writing a cycle of twelve poems covering the span of a year.

Getting published is always an issue for poets. With our website *Berkshire Fine Arts* that was not a problem. Once posted, there was the risk factor of potential embarrassment.

The opposite proved to be true as there was an immediate and sustained response, mostly from friends and colleagues.

Accordingly what started as a whim has evolved into a sustained and energizing project.

Because I lacked an in-depth knowledge of poetry and literature, this has been an adventure of invention. The works follow no familiar form other than a vague notion of free verse. The approach was distilled from decades of experimentation with

Gonzo Journalism, which largely has meant reducing experiences to lists of quick riffs in the manner of jazz improvisation.

Those who receive my emails know them for one sentence graphs: punching out lines stripped to the essence; telling the story with the fewest possible words; grabbing and holding the attention of a reader; composing in a frenzy of inspiration.

My colleague Larry Murray observed how Gonzo Journalism evolved into the staccato style of single sentence paragraphs. That morphed into these works, which he identifies as Gonzo Poetry.

As an undergraduate I loved listening to the recordings of Dylan Thomas as well as Gertrude Stein and T.S. Eliot. At Brandeis I participated in a production of *Under Milk Wood*. I attended a reading by e e Cummings and loved Lawrence Ferlinghetti, who I also heard. Later I met and interviewed Allen Ginsberg who was part of a Beat show I curated for Suffolk University. The poet and photographer Gerard Malanga is a mentor and friend. *Howl* and *On the Road* were important works for me, which I passed along to my students. Reading through Hemingway taught me a lot about mean and lean writing. Standing over my shoulder Bill Cardoso hammered me into shape. Albert Camus was another mentor along with Sappho, Catullus, and François Villon.

Often these poems reflect stories told over a lifetime, perhaps carried in the head for a few days turned over and refined, then blurted out in less than an hour, sometimes several in quick succession. One story often evokes another and then another.

Most of these quick bursts are based on shards, fragments of life experience. They range from family stories and childhood memories to professional encounters with musicians and a career in the arts.

In bits and pieces the poems have been a process of recovering and telling of my life both private and public. A poet friend observed that he has been recovering a mostly unhappy childhood through images from mine.

During a dialogue with a friend, I asked why on earth anyone would be interested in stories of my life? The response was that all lives are interesting if told well and if they touch on basic issues of humanity.

Although I feel that my style is unique and original, others tell me that it's not. I am told of authors to read and explore. Here and there I have glanced at them but am not interested in research. My commitment to poetry is primarily in the writing as well as in the sharing. I have invited and encouraged others to use *Berkshire Fine Arts* as a vehicle. It pleases me to post their work. From its inception in 2006, Astrid Hiemer and I have always viewed *Berkshire Fine Arts* as a platform for a broad range of contributors. We are deeply committed to that mandate.

For the most part these works reflect positive and upbeat moments. That has been deliberate. It is an attempt to take back a childhood and memories of family life that were vilified by devastating accusations. I have shared in this recovery process with my wise, spiritual, forgiving, and loving sister Mary-Louise, aka Pippy.

Adolescence brought a significant change to what had been a happy and privileged childhood. My Sicilian father felt that girls, that is Josephine and Pip, were to be sheltered, protected, and spoiled, where boys were to be beaten, denied, and toughened for manhood.

That resulted in an Oedipal cycle with the twist that even Mom wasn't always there for me. It led to anger, defiance, and destructive behavior. With difficulty I learned not to play the blame game but to take responsibility for my life.

The turning point for the better occurred twenty years ago. I had just bought a three-decker in East Boston. It was an ordeal to get there. In many ways it was the last gasp of gonzo years of drugs, sex, and rock 'n' roll.

When we started dating, Astrid asked if I was willing to change. It had been fun, with no regrets, but she offered something new and different. Having the focus, commitment, and energy to complete this book of poems is just one example of the many adventures and projects we continue to share.

Acknowledgments

The input and critical support of many individuals have made possible this book of poetry.

Most of the poems have been distilled from stories told too many times. For the past twenty years my wife, Astrid Hiemer, has heard them all. She has been the first reader, often out loud to me, of all of the work written for our site *Berkshire Fine Arts*. Frequently this entails catching mistakes, as well as suggestions for improvement. Every writer appreciates another set of eyes, particularly when so astute. I have served in a similar capacity for her postings and projects.

Going back to college years, I have written poetry. Some of it survives in drawing books. At one point I trashed a thick file of work and more or less stopped after that, then I resumed when first using a computer.

Last summer, on a whim, I composed a poem about August. It got a positive response. After I had posted a few more poems, I was surprised by an offer of a reading by the art historian, Keith

Shaw, the director of the Rudd Museum of Art in North Adams. The idea seemed premature based on just a few pieces. That launched a commitment to write at least a hundred over the next six months. This book is the result of that effort and the plan has been to produce this book in time for the reading. Hopefully it will be followed by others.

As a relative stranger to the art form I have had misgivings about writing poetry. Indeed, is it poetry? Surely it is not like my notions of poetry. In particular, I have been sensitive to the generous critical comments of poets and writers.

Remarkably their comments have been generous, supportive, and insightful. I expressed my concerns to Gerard Malanga. He was straightforward in encouraging me to stick to my own instincts. Jane Hudson, a friend since the 1960s, an active poet, artist, and musician, has commented on many posted works.

The poets Geoffrey Movius and Stephen Rifkin have suggested ways in which the poems might be improved. Indeed, the intensity of producing a body of work has been a stimulus and learning curve. One would like to think the work gets better just by practicing an art form. Each poem, in a sense, is a challenge and fresh start.

The critic and writer Larry Murray, publisher of *Berkshire On Stage and Screen*, has been a consistent sounding board. We often meet and discuss aspects of the craft of criticism. Those dialogues have been a give and take for both of us.

My most intensive dialogues have been with Robert Henriquez. We share a passion for jazz and often undertake winter projects of listening and comparing. An example of this was a season of surveying and sharing early New Orleans music with Robert and John Douglas Thompson, an actor preparing to play Louis Armstrong in a one-man play by Terry Teachout.

After that season of "trad," we followed with one on the avant-garde from Cecil Taylor to Sun Ra, Ornette Coleman, Anthony

Braxton, John Coltrane, Chick Corea, and others. The reading for that project was *Blues People* by Leroy Jones, as he was known before becoming Amiri Baraka. Thompson also read that book as part of the seminar.

Always an informed critical thinker, Henriquez has contributed a remarkable essay for this book. He places the work in a context of a mix of Language Poets, Beat, and Gonzo. I am amazed at how uniquely he has captured and described my inspiration and creative process. Truly, he is my soul brother and travel companion.

As a critic, I am fascinated by the creative process, particularly when stretching the limits beyond the comfort zone of my own academic training in art history and the fine arts. This has resulted in a remarkable relationship with the playwright Mark St. Germain. When he is producing new works for Barrington Stage we always meet for breakfast at Dottie's. There has also been an ongoing email dialogue including his rich comments on the subject matter of specific poems.

Many of the poems deal with difficult and complex family history. I have shared wonderful conversations about this material with my sister Mary-Louise "Pippy" Giuliano. It has allowed for recovering positive memories of our childhood.

In bringing this book to completion I am truly indebted to the writer Leanne Jewett. In addition to editing the manuscript and preparing it for publication, she has also walked me through the many complex steps of the business and marketing aspects of publication. The design of this book has been created by Amanda Hill of Studio Two in Lenox, Massachusetts. It was a pleasure to work closely with her.

Beyond Gonzo

An Essay by
J.M. Robert Henriquez
Written for *Shards of a Life*
By Charles Giuliano
2015

As a polymath and critic, Charles Giuliano is defined by a voracious appetite for universal knowledge and the willingness to inform his readers. As a poet, he is defined by language. The poems in *Shards of a Life*, his first book of poetry, are a testament to this double identity. Polymath Giuliano, "having learned much," spans a significant number of different life experiences to have an existential moment. Giuliano the poet seeks the language capable of telling what he has lived, and to this end he is compelled to recast the rules. The subjects in these poems riff and shift, verse lines break and divide (enjambment). Cascades of words in disarray intentionally collide into a staccato rhythm. The outcome is a hugely clever poetry replete with puns, enumerations, antithesis, and other devices.

A characteristic of contemporary time has been its preoccupation with brevity and ephemerality: here today, gone tomorrow—instant communication—speed dating—step right up—act now or never. Readers of the collected poems in *Shards of a Life* must fight against such impulses and go off a different tack.

Giuliano takes to heart the adage "Brevity is the soul of wit." The terse, minimalist style fits the poems beautifully. The poems may be short in length, but they insist on the reader's time and contemplation. They are imbued with a beneficent accessibility that plays well as a contemporary device to retool the reader's attention span.

What exactly is this poetry? It is telling the story, gonzo style, with an excessive economy of words. It is a tug-of-war between lyrical intimacy and analytical distance. It also mirrors the tension between the poet's appreciation of the magic of language and his knowledge of its limitations. Eventually it boils down to an upbeat mix of poetics: two measures of Language poetry, one of Beat and half a measure of Gonzo shine shaken not stirred; *et voilà*, a Charles Giuliano poetic cocktail, somewhat whimsical and playful—but it calls for serious play.

Language poetry may be the operating word here. It can be described this way:

"Key aspects of language poetry include the idea that language dictates meaning rather than the other way around. Language poetry also seeks to involve the reader in the text, placing importance on reader participation in the construction of meaning. By breaking up poetic language, the poet is requiring the reader to find a new way to approach the text."—A Brief Guide to Language Poetry 2004, Academy of American Poets

Language poet Lyn Hejinian comments further on the role of language in writing:

"Language is nothing but meanings, and meanings are nothing but a flow of contexts. Such contexts rarely coalesce into images, rarely come to terms. They are transitions, transmutations, the endless radiating of denotation into relation."—The Language of Inquiry

Other important language poets are: Bob Perelman, Charles Bernstein, and Barrett Watten.

Charles Olson wrote: *"The chain of memory is resurrection"*— the opening verse of a poem. The quote accounts for so much of life's forgotten moments that it demands our full attention. *Shards of a Life*, a book of poetry born on a whim, is set to do just that. Let us rappel down the chain of memory, measure the life span of a man, pick up shards of that life and resurrect them piece by piece. Charles Giuliano—his life—is the archeological site. His book, *Shards of a Life* is the interactive map of that site. The poems are the markers strewn across the site. We, the readers, are the archeologists collecting the shards, sable brush in hand dusting away the sands of forgetfulness.

A life examined is a life lived.

Jean Michel Robert Henriquez is a Multimedia Artist and Broadcast Media Professional who relocated from New York City to the Berkshires. His broadcasting career at the CBS Television Network spanned more than twenty years. Henriquez subsequently worked in Integrated Advertising (Broadcast, Online, and Print) as a freelance Media Consultant and Art Director/Producer.

Family

Charles, Mom, and Josephine 1941.

Great grandparents Patrick
and Nora Nugent of Rockport.

Charles pointing at Windsor Castle
with Mom, Dad, and Pip.

Charles and Josephine with
baby sister Pippy in 1949.

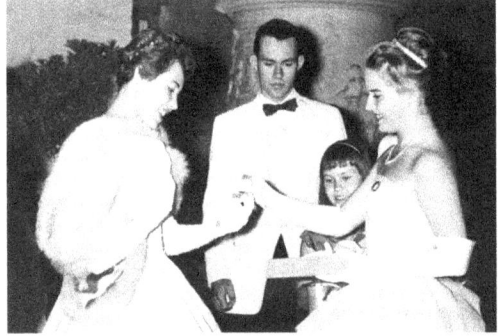

Josephine presented a gift at Versailles
with Charles and Pip looking on.

Maternal grandparents saloonkeeper James Flynn and Josephine in Gloucester 1910.

My family 1940s.

Family Annisquam 1949.

The Giulianos Fred, Dad, Bill, and Albert with Mary, one of four sisters.

Undocumented

Palermo
Loading ships
Hid
Past Gibraltar
Knocked on the captain's cabin
I'm Andrea Giuliano and I want to go to America
They played chess
Talked of hopes and dreams
Docked in New York
Streets paved with gold
Cover of night
Over the side
Sold fruit in Brooklyn
Sent for Maria
Started a family
Never became a citizen
Proud legacy

Grandparents Andrew "Nano" and Maria Giuliano.

Honeymoon

Assisted
Kitchen table
Home delivery
Brooklyn
Followed by a movie
First date
Swarthy arrogant surgeon
Bellevue Hospital resident
Blonde Boston intern
Coney Island Hospital
Following week proposed
Stunned
There had been suitors
None as sincere
Her mom and sister took the train
Simple ceremony
Catskills for a weekend honeymoon
Fired rifles at tin cans
Back to the city on Monday
Dropped her off at the dorm
Drove home to his mother
Eventually
Home and office
On Clinton Street
First born Josephine
Third so named
Then me
Relocated to Brookline
War years
Took over home and practice
Of former boyfriend

They started over
Keeping his promise
For love

Mom and Dad wedding day October 1, 1933.

Mom and Dad as newlyweds late 1930s.

Mom and Dad Gloucester 1940s.

Mom and Dad in formal attire.

Gypsy

Great Depression
Brooklyn storefront
Dad delivered baby
Later came to collect
Gypsies celebrating
Music, food and dancing
Doc come in enjoy
Eat and drink
Let's not talk money
Come back tomorrow
Next day
Knocked but no answer
Looked in the window
Empty

Sicilian Doctor

Knock late at night
Clinton Street, Brooklyn
Mom and baby sister
Asleep
Gangsters
One of them wounded
Doc you gotta help us
Just stitch him up
Now and then we bring you something
Whatever you need
Do us a favor
Get out of my house
Closed the door
Sweating bullets

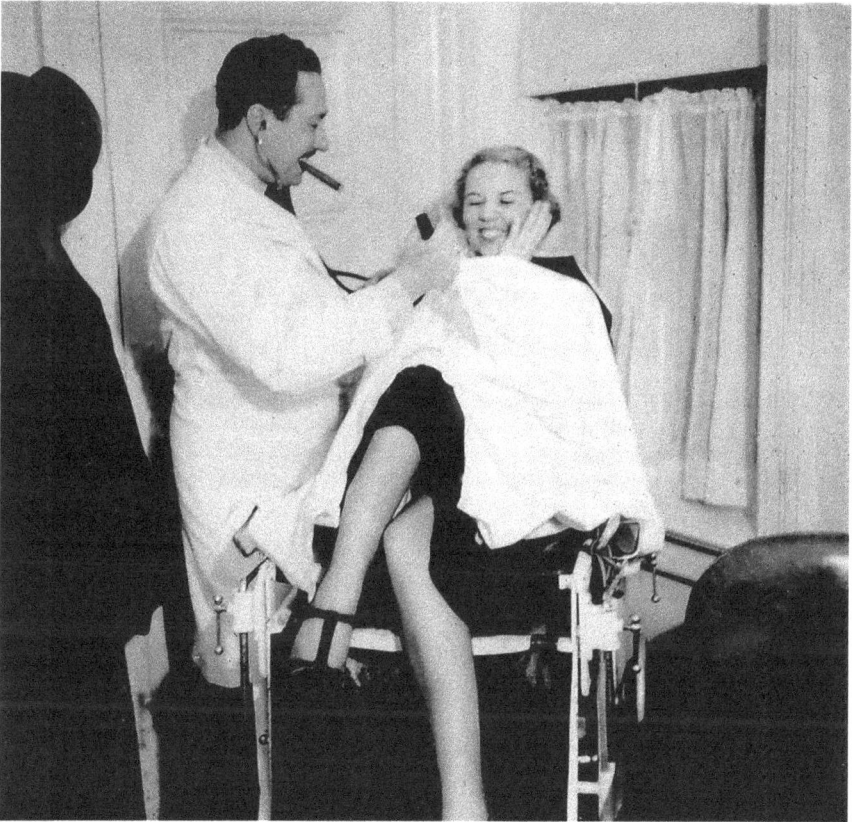

Dad with cigar treating a patient in Brooklyn.

Coney Island

Intern
Harbor Hospital
Mom rode the ambulance
Slept in uniform
Minutes to ring the bell
Off to emergencies
Drowning on the beach
Mob hits
Jail runs
Junkie needing a fix
Screaming
Mom gave him a taste
Calmed down
Hour later called back
Driver said
Hey Doc ask him what's his dose
Give it to him
Or we'll be back and forth all night
He knew more than she did
They made
A great team

Dr. Josephine R. Flynn riding the ambulance Harbor Hospital 1930s.

Thanksgiving

1940s
All safe
Uncles home from war
Thanksgiving
Like Norman Rockwell
Under the Tiffany chandelier
Sprawling Allston home
Wraparound porches
Huge gardens with rhubarb
Flynn Grandparents
He puffing on a pipe
Amazed
Dish towel
Perfectly good
Over the roasting bird
Keeps it moist explained
Gathered round
Blessings
Grandpa deferring to
Dad the surgeon
Carving deftly
The kid
I got a drumstick

Grandparents James and Josephine Flynn.

Wake

Visiting Allston
Bonnie Prince Charlie
Best & Company outfits
Grandpa Flynn in huge kitchen
Dressing gown
Puffing on pipe
Wet dishcloth thrown in my face
Ritual greeting
Scary but loving
Great laughter
Breaking usual silence
Said little
Like Will Rogers
Only knew what he read in newspapers
Bootlegger, hotel and saloon keeper
The Kennedys
That other Irish clan
Coffin in the parlor
Surrounded by potted palms
House full of mourners
Eating turkey sandwiches
Slopping down oceans of whiskey
Raucous merriment
Rite of passage
Friends neighbors and perfect strangers
A right fine man he was
Come to pay respects
Cold and stiff mostly ignored
Puzzled me
Hadn't yet read James Joyce
All so strange

Missing Grandpa
No wet laughter this time
A Last Hurrah

Grandfather James Flynn.

Pasta

During the War
Dad had a plan to survive
In the event of bombing
Or invasion
Of Brookline
Pasta
In the basement
Dark scary room
Clutter of dusty stuff
On shelves
Cases of canned tomato and paste
Gallons of olive oil
Feeding the family
Into the 1950s
While cooking
Go get me a can of this or that
Lasted until the 1960s
British Invasion
Beatles on Ed Sullivan
No urgent need for
Spaghetti

My father Dr. Charles and grandmother Maria with pooch.

Christmas Shopping

Mom started in August
Stashing away
Dad waited until the last minute
Took us to the mall at Chestnut Hill
In the 1950s quite a marvel
All those downtown stores
In the burbs
Huge parking lots
We advised
Ostrich leather purse one year
Solitaire
Diamond as big as the Ritz
The next
The engagement ring she never had
Married in a rush
Great Depression
Dad got cash at the bank
Stack of red envelopes
A case of Scotch
In Holiday boxes
Christmas morning
All Mom's presents
From Santa actually
They were up all night in the basement
Banging away assembling toys
He drove me to the hospital
Picked up huge cooked turkey
Thelma's famous pies
Then like a paper route
Drove around to his feeders
The G.P.'s

Handed me a bottle and envelope

Knock on that door

Tell them this is from Dr. Giuliano

Men in undershorts and bathrobes

Glanced out at the Caddy

Waves and smiles

The spirit of giving

Strange lessons

Trimming the Tree

Dad Jo and Me
Drove from Brookline to Framingham
Along Route 9
Outdoor markets
Tons of trees
Looking for the fullest
Twirling them about
Viewed from all angles
Nice fat one
Tied to the roof of the car
In the living room
Too tall
Top hacked off with a kitchen knife
Base too fat for the stand
Puffing at a cigar
Dad sweating and chopping
Finally upright
Branches pulled down and arranged
Barest side in the back
Sappy oozing resin wafting through the room
Dad now retired to observe and instruct
Boxes up from the basement
Ancient candles in all the windows
Lights plugged in
Some not working
Clever Jo soldering with lead tinsel
Flash and sparks
Voila
Let there be light
First draped around evenly
Then the garlands

Tinsel placed strand by strand
Impatiently I chucked it freestyle
Finally the antique balls
Dad made eggnog
With nutmeg and whipped cream
Driving by our house ablaze
In dark Brookline
Celebrating Hanukah

Christmas in Brookline 1940s.

Woolworths

Coolidge Corner
Streetcar ride or long walk
Woolworths
Christmas presents
Cheap but inventive
Saved up allowance
For being good and doing chores
Huge bottle of perfume for Mom
Fascinating and faceted
Better on looks than scent
For little Pip
Mechanical cars and pups
Lots of them
She was just a squirt
Played with her after school
Inventive games
Ran the little car over her tender head
Hair got caught in the gears
Impulsively yanked it off
With a hunk of scalp
Crying
I'm telling Mom and Dad
Begged her not to
She did
They freaked
Years later
Off my conscience
On the phone today reminded her
Talked about writing this poem
Why not she said
Water under the bridge
More like Niagara Falls

Family portrait with Donner.

Chocolates

Glancing with amusement
In the waiting room
Annual Christmas visit
North End to Brookline
By trolley
Worlds apart
Paisans
The old Sicilian with his wife
Large peasant hands
Clutching that huge box of chocolates
Biggest imaginable
Not the best quality
More the immensity of salvation
Tribute for a life saved
Omerta
For you Doc
An offer
He could not refuse

Casatta

Holidays
Sicilians came from Brooklyn
Not allowed in the house
Without Casatta
Built with rum-soaked sponge cake
Cannoli filling
Glazed frosting
Top covered with candied fruit
In the center preserved orange
Surrounded by white lattice
Supporting a sugared rose
Must be from Monteleone's
Or Tardo's
Fruit removed to a separate plate
Agony over thickness of slices
Amount of fruit
Cordials and espresso with Sambuca
Tales of the cake
Adventures of getting there
Italian spoken laughingly
Lasted a couple of days
Slices less generous
Fruit more sparing
Cake drying out
Filling touching on sour
Sunset over the Mediterranean
Until next year
Now long gone

Cigars

Family trip to Europe
Bal a Versailles
Mom packed for months
Gowns for the ladies
Tails for men
Last minute
Dad opened a suitcase
Tossed in
Shirts and socks
Boxes of cigars
Customs officials
Mean little twits with caps
Wanted to tax cigars
Ranted and raged
Wouldn't budge
Gallic huffs and puffs
Waved a wad of C Notes
No dice
Next plane home
Oh Dad we pleaded
No cigars then basta
With a shrug
Suitcases slammed shut
Chalk X
On to Paris
The almighty dollar
Spoke French

Escorting Josephine at the Bal a Versailles.

Barge

Canal in Venice
1950s
Dad sketching
Noon
Workers staring at him
What's wrong he asked
Maestro
When will you be finished
We have to move the barge
Lunch in a trattoria
New friends
Street Cleaner
That first family trip
With Dad
Standing on the curb
Waiting to cross

Street Cleaner

Snail's pace

Sweeping

A breeze

Blowing debris

Frantic call for help

People jumping on flying papers

Standing like statues

Waiting for calm

Grazie Mille

Silently moved on

Went back to work

Amazed

Have a cigar Dad said

When in Rome

Cure

For the old woman
On welfare
Mom prescribed
Medicinal whiskey
One shot daily
Too soon
Wanted a refill
What happened
Oh Doctor Flynn
She said in a flutter
Me heart
Hurtin' bad
Near the end of me
Prayed to the Virgin
She answered
Quick Bridget
The bottle
Saved me life

1932

Mom middle of second row Middlesex College of Medicine and Surgery,
later Brandeis University, 1932.

Mom presenting a trophy 1930s.

Cottage Industry

Anniversary week
Sandwich
Dense rows
Cottages on the Cape
Marsh walks
To the tip
Curved around to ocean
Day trips
Nearby Barnstable
Whale watch
Humpbacks feeding
Bulking for winter
Making calves
In the Caribbean
Busy days
Reading and writing
Afternoons exploring
Sunset cruise in Osterville
Russell and family
Gliding past mansions
Mega-estates
Celebrities and old families
Koch bought DuPont's water frontage
Some $65 million from here to there
Homes hung with Monet and Renoir
Shown at the MFA
Dinner at Daniel Webster Inn
Recalling wedding day
Mom and sisters two hours early
Astrid still cleaning
Minister 90 minutes late

Hot September day
Backyard East Boston
Under the apple tree
Toasts like roasts
Exhausted
Back to work
Monday morning
Good times
Two decades on

Anniversary week in Sandwich on Cape Cod.

Dancing Shoes

Annual Holiday dinner
National Arts Club
Elegant New York mansion
Uncle Bill Giuliano and Estere
Now 86
Just stopped teaching
Romance languages
Queens College
Swims every day
Slipped and fell recently
Slick soles of shoes
Billo, let me take them to the cobbler
Rubber soles for
Better grip
They do a good job
Bill agreed
Except not these
She asked why
For dancing
They laughed softly
Formerly an instructor at Arthur Murray
Reservations for New Year's Eve
Gliding the night away
December 17, 1999

My uncle Dr. Bill Giuliano enjoyed dancing into his 90s.

Youth

Representing Mt. Alvernia Academy on WCOP's Quizdown.

Assisted Ready-Made

After a bath Mom loved
Guerlain's Talcum Powder
Stumped for a present
Charged one at Mr. Jacob's drugstore
He wrapped it nicely
Too expensive for my allowance
She was pleased
Until the bill came
Following year
I would love something you make
Out in the alley behind our house
Found a nice big rock
Cleaned it up real good
Painted a head of Santa on it
Wrapped it best I could
Not easy
Handed it over
Christmas morning
Beaming with pride
How wonderful she said
What is it
A doorstop

Relic

After lunch
Chapel
Mt. Alvernia Academy
The nuns thrilled
Announced a visiting relic
Saint so and so
One by one we approached the altar
Gold object
Shaped like a crucifix
Small glass window
Behind which
Tiny fragment
Body parts
Hacked up for
Thousands of reliquaries
Churches around the world
Medieval pilgrimages
Canterbury Tales
Grace and forgiveness
Prayers for miracles
Kneeling
Thrust toward my lips
Eyeballed it intently
Seeing is believing
Priest in vestments
Kissed
Then a quick swipe
Holy cloth
Back to a pew

Radiating bliss
Bursting out for
Recess
And more sins

Divine Wind

Prayers before recess
Heads bowed
Nuns watching
Cut one
Middle of Hail Marys
Silent but deadly
Venial sin
Happened again
Day after day
Asked Mom a doctor
For anti-fart pills
She had something for anything
Try these
Medication and meditation
Worked miracles
Divine intervention
Turned off the gas

Stairway to Heaven

A kid

Visiting New York with Mom

Exploring wonders

Rockefeller Center skaters

Broadway for Brigadoon

Chatting with Duke and Duchess of Windsor

Empire State Building

Looking up as far as one can see

Tallest building in the world

Entering the lobby

Elevators

Several as I recall

One after another

Higher and higher

A little scared

Never liked small closed spaces

Out at the top

Dizzy terrace

Whipping wind

Vertigo

Fear of being blown off

Cautiously approaching the edge

Gazing out and down

High as one could be

Other than an airplane

Reached up to

Touch the sky

Royal Pain

Just a squirt
NY with Mom and Sis
Before Caribbean Cruise
S. S. Brazil
Dinner at Mamma Leone's
Before Broadway
Iced celery and olives
Perusing the enormous menu
Lobster Fra Diavolo
Over linguini
I liked lobster
It didn't like me
Mom I don't feel so good
Racing for the ladies' room
Prepubescent
Projectile vomit
Wiping out a large table
Sounds of mayhem
Gasping night air
Let's go back to the hotel
You'll be OK
Doctor Mom always right
Recovered
Orchestra for Brigadoon
See that man
Armed with program and pen
Ask for his autograph
Approaching reluctantly
Flanked by elegant ladies
In evening gowns
Smiling at me seductively

Adorable child
So I'm told
Please Sir may I have your autograph
The Duke frowned imperiously
Wallace Simpson clutched his arm
If you wish to have my autograph
Come to my suite at the Waldorf Astoria
Where we were staying
I imagined soda and sweets
Tête-à-tête
Mom was emphatic
You're not going
Never explained why

Kiss

Pretty and smart
Shelia Murphy
Always one step ahead of me
Just out of reach
Quicker with answers
First in the class
Me always second
No matter what
Came to school one day
Blonde hair in a net
Like Scarlett O'Hara
On school bus
Lunged
Declaring love demanding a kiss
Gorilla moment
Next day
Entire school marched into auditorium
Mother Superior
Truly terrifying
Boys and girls
Something terrible has happened
Moment of suspense then shock
Charles Giuliano kissed Shelia Murphy
Uproar
Hero to some villain to others
For a week
Nuns rode the bus
Boys on one side girls the other
First true love
Utter catastrophe

Bullies

Angelo Treniello was smart

Chubby and obedient

Did his homework

No good at sports

His only friend Murray

Smallish and wimpy

One day I played with them

Nobody else did

Making snowmen

Older boys

Ran down the hill smashing them

Biggest one confronted me

Shoved and slapped

Clocked and knocked him cold

Not a peep from the nuns

Pissed

After Mt. Alvernia and nuns
Boston Latin School was tough
On every level
First year
Class Six
Nobody, Sixie a nothing
Room for thirty-six
Eight standing
By Thanksgiving a row of empty desks
That June even fewer
Trying to make friends
Taking a pee
Slates with streaming water
Slapped Nixon on the back
Friendly gesture
Lurched forward hand getting wet
Turned around pissing on me
Told him to stop
Warned him adding
No Latin School boy strikes another Latin School boy
He didn't listen
One punch in the gut
Fell and broke his arm
Dragged to the principal's office
The fearsome Mr. McKim
Censured and sent home in tears
Dad called the office and explained
Mr. McKim showed up in homeroom
Asked the class
Has anyone seen Mr. Nixon urinate on another Latin School boy
Dead silence

He asked again

Has anyone seen Mr. Nixon go to the bathroom on another boy

Chorus of responses

Off the hook

He wrote into my record

Action that any red-blooded Latin School Boy would take

The Game

Ancient rivalry
Boston Latin vs. Boston English
Harvard Stadium
Thanksgiving
In the stands
Me and a mate
Dorchester girls
Sat down
Cozied up
Sweet smiles
Took my arm
Cuddled
Bitter cold morning
Hands freezing
No gloves
Warm them here
Sliding between her thighs
Light gray wool pants
Toasty and sensual
Looking about nervously
Forbidden fruit
Feverish excitement
Lost focus
Think we won
Walked her to the bus
Slow and romantic
Never got her number
Lived too far away

Another world in fact
Raced home for dinner
How was the game
Oh great

Tack

Bobby Dangelmeyer
Best friend
Bitter rival
Had the fastest Fish Boat
Local catboats
Always first around the buoys
Fleet just followed
Running out
Rounding the mark
Tacking home
Tricky up the Squam River
Races won or lost
Against the tide
Clusters of boats
Anchored to bathe at
Wingaersheek Beach
Competition for second or third
Final turn
Bobby tacked port offshore
Toward Ipswich River
They all followed
Rick Lordan and I took starboard
All alone
Headed straight for the lighthouse
Catching an offshore breeze
Pointing up ever higher
Laying a line for the channel
Watched the fleet
Falling ever farther astern
Took the cannon
Stowed the boat

On the club porch

Saw Bobby finish

Second

Followed by the fleet

Always take the other tack

Lose most times

Now and then

Win big

Regatta

Squam Day
Annual regatta
Chowder Race
Catered by Woodman's of Essex
Served in enamel pans
Donut on the handle
Star Boats sailing over from Rockport's Sandy Bay
A tow from Conomo Point
Yachts from as far away as Marblehead
Fleet setting sail
Lightnings, Fish Boats, Turnabouts
Rigged and tacking to starting line
Off the Annisquam Lighthouse
In the open bay
Cup for all over fastest craft
Competitions by class
From up river they came at race time
Brothers
Old timers in linen suits
One at the tiller
Other hiking out trimming sails
Brims of straw hats bent back by the breeze
An apparition
Like an Eakins or Homer painting
Ancient gaff rigged sloop
Long and thin like a canoe
Flying by at a furious clip
Finished the course in record time
Then poof
Gone in the salt mist of memory

In Annisquam one sails or plays tennis.

Race Week

Highlight of the summer
Marblehead Race Week
Tow from Annisquam
Raucous fun
Finding a space to anchor
Harbor clustered with yachts
Every kind of craft
Gathered to compete
Waiting for the launch
Hanging on the porch
Corinthian Yacht Club
Busy starting line
Hanging back
Waiting for your class
Split-second timing
Not jumping the gun
Strategies for best position
That day blustery gusts
White caps
Many capsized
Towed home
Strong winds
Leveled playing field
Best skippers prevailed
Over faster boats
Bobby and me racing home
Splitting tacks
Inching ahead
Lining up final move
Calculated to catch the line
Precisely

Nicking the buoy
On starboard with right of way
He crashing for Ricky and me on port
Yelling Starboard, Starboard
Kept coming hard
Furious look
Hating to get beaten
Avoiding collision
Came about
He tacked and got the cannon
Back on land
Launched protest
No need
They saw it all
Appalled
Still have the trophy
Dark victory

Pearl Diving

Summer job
Annisquam Yacht Club
Built on piles and piers
Hovering over eel grass
Marsh and tides
Restaurant
Members only
Started as a waiter
Cheap Yankees
Ordered Chopped Steak
Never tipped
Opted for the kitchen
Afternoons prepping
Worked for Eleanor
Made the salads
Got lobsters from trap
Drove her home
Back to wash dishes
On busy weekends
Late into the night
Friends dropped by
Partying
Got crazy as time dragged on
Window next to the sink
Washed one tossed one
Cheers and laughter
Well-kept secret
Fear of low tide
Shards of youth

Elvis

Baby blue Cadillac convertible

White calf leather seats

Bluewall tires

Gold spoke rims

Sweet ride

Occasionally borrowed

Hot dates

Anguished father greeted me

Got the lookover

Head to heels

Called upstairs

Sweetheart

Elvis

Is here

All shook up

See Section

Annisquam 1950s
Sultry summer night
Dad tired
Emergency call
Please take me
Chance to drive the Cadillac
Parked outside to wait
No, come in
Locker room
Doctors changing into scrubs
Idle chatter
Nurse poked in
Patient ready for delivery
Go watch Dad said
Reluctantly
Woman in agony
Never again she moaned
Out it popped all wet and screeching
Staggered down the hall
Standing in front of a huge fan
Catching my breath
Dr. Giuliano the OR is ready
Come along he insisted
You'll be doing this some day
Another pregnant woman
Out cold
Belly flanked by towels
Swabbed with Mercurochrome
Hovering cowering back
Come closer
Haven't scrubbed
You're not touching anything

Stand next to me

Scalpel held like a conductor's baton

His renowned bikini cut

Cut clamp cut clamp

Instruments flying

Decisive moment he said

Paused

Reached in and scooped

Baby came up

Delivery double-header

Gaping wound of blood

Sound of suction

I went down

Came to surrounded by nurses

Are you OK

Fine

How's the baby

Drove home

Dawn broke

Birth trauma

Freshman English

Arnie Sugarman
A grad student
Taught Freshman English
Often late
Or skipped
When he did teach
Pretentious bore
Ersatz Oxford accent
Mumbled profundities
Smoked a pipe
In class
Being in college was
Scary but fun and exciting
Camus' The Stranger
Thrilled
Inspired series of drawings
For an assignment
Wrote like that
Best I could
Short deadpan sentences
My grandfather's funeral
Family gathered in Brooklyn
Rose the eldest daughter
Leaping into the grave with Pop
Held back
Having survived
Hosted family feast
Rare encounter with
The Sicilians
That essay
In embryo

What I do now
Birth of Gonzo
Crushed by a C-Plus
Lived to write another day

Premed

Mom and Dad were doctors
Expected
No demanded same of me
Family business
Freshman year
Flunked chemistry
A in art
Makeup C+ Harvard Summer School
No fun
Hated labs
In August
Announced plan to major in art
No way
Dragged into backyard
Shirts ripped off
Sense beaten into me
Fists flew
Wanted to kill him
Tough Sicilian loved boxing
Separated
Won't pay for college
Mom threatened divorce
OK but without my blessing
The curse
On your own
You will never marry
Never have children
Never own your own home
Then we had spaghetti
That day
I became an artist

Smashing

IFIF

55 Kenwood Avenue, Newton, Mass.

Headquarters 1960s

Tim Leary and Richard Alpert

Visiting

Bruce Conner

Artist

Offered old Remington typewriter

Declined

I'm an artist no need for it

Left saying nothing

Returned with baseball bat

Smashed it to smithereens

Ribbon reels rolling angrily across floor

Lower East Side

Couple of years later

303 East 11th Street

No phone

Jim Jacobs dropped by

Have a typewriter in the car

Yours

An omen

Started typing

Have been

Ever since

Romance

Broken heart
Poor prospect
Yet again
Girlfriends moved on
Life of an artist
Not much of a provider
Mom said
Romance without finance
Ain't
Got no chance

Kites

Easter Sunday
They fly kites in Bermuda
There for spring break
Brought the Modern Lovers
With Cambridge neighbor
Arthur Gallagher
Inverurie
Family hotel
With his mom
Drove to holiday celebration
Large house other end of island
Nice digs
Descendants of pirates and marooned criminals
The Colonies
Hostess eyeballed me in the kitchen
Gazing askance at hipster bandito
Long hair huge stash
Oh she said
In a Margaret Dumont manner
Me as Groucho
And where are your people from
Talked of Irish ancestors in Gloucester
The Nugent clan
Pregnant daughter-in-law asked
Is your mother Doctor Josephine Flynn
Surprised
Answered yes
You're my second cousin
Onlooker said
Oh the dowager gasped
Go fly a kite

LAX

First trip to LA
Elton John party
On the plane
Howard Zinn
Dissident
Entering terminal
Loudspeaker
Mr. Giuliano
Your limousine is waiting
Scuse me Howie
Gotta go
What do you want to see
Yours for the day

Elton John, Al Kooper, reporter David Felton, and Charles Giuliano in Hollywood.

Rolling Stone reporter David Felton dubbed Charles Harry Bikes. Barry Savenor photo.

1940

The Class of 1940
Me
Jane Hudson, Steve Nelson, Jaune Quick-to-See Smith
Turning 74
Saturday
October 25
Pretty Fucking Old
But not enough
Nothing really notable
Off year till 75
A Biggie
On the road
No time for celebration or bathos
Astrid bought me a bell
Arcosanti
Lighting candles
In LA
Couple of days hence
She bought one at Frys
Will use it every night plus
Life
On the fly

Correggio in Parma

Kress Foundation Grant
Summer in Italy
Sponsor Professor Binion's
Only request
Parma to see
Dome by Correggio
Reasons why things don't work
Domani, tomorrow
Ciuso, closed
Festa, holiday
Sciopero, strike
Arriving to all of the above
Ghost town
Slammed shut
Found the church
Looked up at the dome
Dark as a coal mine
Spotted the coin box
Cento lire
No moneta
Scarce that summer
Pockets empty
Sitting alone dejected
Tourists entered
Looked up
Harry give me a hundred lire coin
Miracolo
Let there be light
Three glorious minutes
Priest arrived tending to the altar
Scusi padre

Si si mon filio

Correggio e importante non e vero?

Ah, si si mon filio

Molto molto importante

Ma il cupola e scuro, perchè?

Curtains over the windows

Ma non capisce mon filio

Iffa you no cover the windows

You no getta the cento lire

God is love

For a price

Italia

Music

Miles playing softly with a Harmon mute. Charles Giuliano photo © 2015.

Trane

Speedway Gang

Descended on

Jazz Workshop

No cover standing at the bar

Trane wailing

Each set one tune

Giant Steps

Wall of sound behind his horn

Clusters of chords from McCoy Tyner

Elvin Jones driving the beat

They left the stand

Trane departed with Lowrider

The man in a kilt

Still on stage

Jimmy Garrison sweating

Played bass forever

Astonishing solo

Trane returned

Went to the bridge

Took it out

Elvin

Rookie reporter
Elvin Jones
Trane's drummer
After the set
Asked club owner
Freddy Taylor
Introduction to Mr. Jones
Pointing
Knock on the door
Entered
Wife pulling off soaked shirt
Elvin wrung it out
Puddle of water
Wow you sweat a lot
Icebreaker
Talked about Trane
Upcoming tour of Japan
Left with notes
First piece as a
Jazz Critic

Rahsaan

Three horns jammed in his mouth
Blowing chords
Never been done before or since
Tsunami
Circular breathing
Nonstop
Roland Rahsaan Kirk
Blind musician explained
Dinner at the Half Shell
Near the gig
Rocking back and forth
Things hanging round his neck
Lots of silver tape
Tactile
Stabbing at food
Wound up
Enraged
Jazz is being ruined
Ranted
Mutha fuckin white critics
The band cracked up
Silently
What's that you say
Mother fucking white critics
Wrote it all down
Sight unseen
Volunteered slavery

Stones

Proofing page
Sunday Showguide
Tabloid insert
Weekly feature
Herald Traveler
Ad for Stones at the Garden
Friday afternoon
Bribed printer
Pulled extra sheet
Called friends
Sent coupon and check
That night
Andy and Jane
Me and date
Section one loge
Awesome seats
Stones Omega Tour
Mick in tall hat and long red scarf
Cavorting on stage
Charlie rock steady
Keith crisp licks
Surrounded by Hells Angels
Security for the tour
Brown paper bag
Joints
Huge
Spliffs
One a Y
Two splayed reefers
Spliced into another
Both ends lit

Took tokes and passed along

Hey man

Staying nervously cool

Thanksgiving

Later

Free Concert

Altamont

Angels busted heads

Fan sent to heaven

Amen

Mick leaps. Charles Giuliano photo © 2015.

Jimi Hendrix

Descended on Broadway club
Cheetah
Paparazzi
Cruising for pictures
Gave me old camera
He's with us
Loaded with film
Pooled and processed
Waved in
Easy
Meet the press
Regulars
Hung out backstage
Curtis Knight and the Flames
Be out front tonight
Turning him loose
Mustang Sally
Broadway soul band
Jive outfits
Cheap leopard print shirts
Jimmy James
Behind the back
Over his head
Picking with teeth
Wailing
Went uptown with pictures
Cheap hotel
Wimpy handshake

Mumbled thanks
Returned from London
Jimi Hendrix
Experienced

Cop Out

Newport Jazz Festival
Press tent
Ushers assembled
Tall redhead
California girl
Wild Strawberry
Matched my kicks
Post concert mansion party
Upstairs
Room Nobby rented
Few z's before posting
Providence Journal
You guys take the bed
He snoozed on broad windowsill
Shots fired
Commotion
Up the fire escape
Half naked guy
Busted through the window
Nobby yelled
Get the fuck out of here
I'll call the cops
Answered
I am a cop
Troopers cavorting below
Smiles of a summer's night

Mississippi

Delivered to my office

Boston Herald Traveler

Old bluesman

Mississippi Fred McDowell

Note pinned to his chest

Directions to the gig

He's yours for the afternoon

Put him in a cab when you're done

Walked to the South End

Deadbeat dive dark and dank

Ginger brandy and beers

He had a few

Must get hot in the summer

Sure nough

How to keep cool

Why youze jus hoists that windah high

All you can do

Tales of Yazoo

Ole Miss

Strange fruit

Blues

Captain Beefheart

Roger I want a lobster
Beefheart said
Huge one at the Half Shell
The rest of us dined modestly
The Captain lived large
Absconded me
Driving around NY in a limo
Discoursing on art and music
Equal interests
A white label test pressing
Clear Spot
Personalized front and back
Magic marker expressionist drawing
Signed Don Van Vliet
Afternoon at Chinese tailor
Shared with friend and mentor
Ornette Coleman
Don played freejazz clarinet
Lovely Jan waiting patiently
California girl
Promised her Dad to live straight
Self taught trained musicians
Zoot Horn Rollo
Rivalry with Zappa
Who produced
Classic album
Trout Mask Replica
Avant-garde rock
Out there
Wrote Sunday features
Never enough

Asked me to join the band

Maybe

Should have

Miss him madly

Captain Beefheart invited Charles to join his band. Charles Giuliano photo © 2015.

Moondog

Viking
Tall, hooded, draped with capes
Staff as the blind man's cane
Knew his Prestige albums
Put money in the cup
Received sheet of poems
Became friends
Daily greeting and chat
Proposed concert at 57th Street gallery
Spectrum
A co-op
Members agreed
Good publicity
Moondog got the gate
Met to plan
Fleabag
Greeted me without the gear
Roach-infested room
Single hanging bulb for rare visitor
Hotplate
Canons and coffee
Watched him suit up
Man into Viking
Radio with Bob Fass
Promoting the gig
Members hung group show
They wanted exposure
His dancer friend
Linda
In costume and face paint
Moved to the beat

He on the floor
Barely visible in packed gallery
Martha Graham up front
Playing his triangular drum
Intricate time signatures
Poetic chants
My introduction
Excuse our rustic appearance
We are after all
Diamonds in the rough
Phil Bleeth just loved that
Not long after
Left New York for Mexico
Never got there

Godfather of Soul

Please Please Please
Drop to the stage
Caped
One more time
Then again
Cold sweat
Fast twirl
Mike stand smashed down
Pulled back
Split
Glide
Midnight
Boston's Sugar Shack
In the Zone
Pimp walk
Floating in
Voguing
Dudes in colors
Mink coats
Fur hats
Bling
Stables of working girls
Night of hoin
Money rolling
Drinks and blow
Superfly
Tight dressing room
James Brown toweled off
White guy
Critic
Asking questions
Entourage

Muscle pressing in
Packing heat
Guttural raspy voice
I shined shoes in front of
Tallest building in Augusta Ga
Now I own that building
Chorus of
Right on
Say it Loud
Tell the man
IRS
Later
Took it all away

James Brown talked about shining shoes as a kid. Charles Giuliano photo © 2015.

Bitches Brew

Lennie's on the Turnpike
Leaving
Columbia's Sal Ingeme chasing after me
Miles wants to talk to you
Jive question
Months of research
Listening to all those albums
What was it like to blow with Bird
Sheeeeet
Raspy whisper
Such a drag to talk about the past
Frustrated
So what do you want to talk about
Did you hear the gig tonight
Michael Henderson, bass; Gary Bartz, horns; Jack de Johnette,
drums; Keith Jarrett, piano; Chick Corea, piano;
John McLaughlin, guitar
Looking in a mirror
Combed his hair
Seeing my reflection
No eye contact
You can help me
OK Miles
I got Keith and Chick
Can't keep 'em both
Who should I get rid of
I don't know
Keeping Keith
Gives me more
Never talked about Bird
Musicians have something to say

Reasons why
Listen and learn
No script
Best interviews

Miles was always challenging. Charles Giuliano photo © 2015.

Mulligan Stew

Baritone sax
Huge horn
Harry Carney in Duke's band
Mulligan played it easy as alto
Long bop lines
Fluid licks
Blue-eyed soul
Line for Lyons
Chet on horn at Carnegie Hall
Classic albums with Desmond
Knocked on the door
Opened a crack
Saw the woman
Not Sandy Dennis
One-nighters
Snapped
Meet me by the elevator
Ride to the lobby
Unleashed tirade
Piped in easy listening
Ersatz Kenny G
Composer ripped off
Screed continued
Angry about everything
Music business
Jazz killed by rock 'n' roll
Finally
What's that got to do with me
Don't even know you
Just writing a piece
Helping the gig

Caught up short
Moment of reflection
Sorry man
Straight talk
No chaser

Gerry Mulligan. Charles Giuliano photo © 2015.

Anita

Day off
Sandy asked
Pick up Anita O'Day at Logan
Explained to Stephanie
Do you mind
Watching at the gate
She got in the middle linking our arms
Driving north stop for a drink
Told her life story
Over martinis
Kicking in Hawaii
On the beach
Sweats and flashes
Into the surf
Cold then hot
Turkey shooting skag
Motel
Where for dinner
Date now scrapped
Check out the club
Weeknight
Lesbian band
Awful music
What time tomorrow for the hairdresser
Errand boy
Take me here get me that
Rehearsals
Pickup trio kids from Berklee
Over and over
Theme song
Antonio Carlos Jobim's Wave

Can't get it right
You're rushing me
Follow me I don't follow you
Counting it off
Drummer fired
Ex husband John Poole flown in
Right beat makes a difference
Opening night
Coiffed and gowned
Give me a joint
My intro
Came on with a nice head
Wave crashing just right
That signature swing night after night
All in the timing
Above, below, around, ahead, behind the beat
No vibrato
Signature flat scat
White heat
Shared a spike with Billie
At Newport
Tea for two
Jazz on a Summer's Day
Long white gloves
Hiding the tracks
Hey Mr. Charlie
Give me a toke
Back to Logan
On to next gig

Errand boy for singer Anita O'Day. Charles Giuliano photo © 2015.

Joe Cocker

The Tea Party
Reporter Tim Crouse in jacket and tie
Rock and roll
Loosen up
Hit the head for a reefer
Guy barged in
Give me a toke man
Later
On stage
Spastic twitching about
Slurring words
I get high with some help from my friends
Upstairs
We smiled

The Mooche

Teenager
Uncle Brother
Took us to see the Duke
Huge fan
Storyville in Copley Square
Free copies of
Newport Jazz Festival catalogue
Prior summer
Beautiful photos
Treasured
Arched walls black brown and beige
Floored by the big band sound
Mood Indigo
Awesome horn section
Opened with Stray's Take the A Train
Between sets
Introduced to Ellington
Trying to get him off the rock 'n' roll kick
Not true
Signed the cheap 10" LP
Only one I had
Bought in a drug store
Still have it
Years later returned the favor
Buddy Rich at Lennie's on the Turnpike
Legendary drummer fronting a band
Tiny dressing room
Buddy stripped to skivvies
Talked of Carson and the Tonight Show
Plans for Vegas
Elegantly dressed

George Frazier on the couch

Off the wagon

Globe columnist's occasional mumble

Buddy listened

Politely

Respect for renowned critic

Dialogue bombed

Back to me

Driving home

Brother was thrilled

You cut Frazier

Last seen that night

Went on a bender

Resurfaced

Weeks Later

Locke Ober's

His usual Finnan Haddie

Sophisticated Lady

Eliot Hotel
Across from Jazz Workshop
Duke Ellington in for the week
Front desk for
Room number
Off elevator down hall
Commotion
Bags flying into the hall
Angry woman
All right for you Duke
Slipping by in a huff
Door of suite open
Spacious room empty
Entering gently softly calling
Duke, Duke, Duke
Grand presence emerged
Elegantly robed
Tied nylon stocking cap
Keeping the process neat
Seated on huge couch
Introductions
Some people can be so rude
Taking notes
What are you doing now
Writing
About
My favorite subject
What's that
Me

Watching me taking notes
That looks like enough
Now I have to put my head
On some feathers

Copenhagen

Standby
Cheap Copenhagen flight
Boston then stops to refuel
Gander, Newfoundland
Iceland middle of the night
Out of the office for a week
Sunday piece due on return
Come back with a story
Telephone book
Called ex-pat Dexter Gordon
What's happening baby
Explained
Meet for lunch
Solid baby
Tall handsome dude
Talked Danish bebop to the waiter
Need a taste to get straight man
Shakes
Frozen schnapps
Joined him keeping pace
A few
The man was after him in the States
Staying alive in exile
Kicking horse
Denmark sweet to hipsters
Staggering to hotel
Like an acid trip
Later backstage US gig
Triumphant return
Signed with Columbia
Tours and festivals
Sweet horn

Horizontal tribute to audience

Lyrical playing

Words spoken then played

Poetic and poignant

Stroking and caressing the music

Hey Dexter remember me

We met in Copenhagen

No baby

Next gig

Hey Dexter remember me

No baby

Again and again

Running gag

Backstage reefer madness

Schnapps with Dexter Gordon in Copenhagen. Charles Giuliano photo © 2015.

Yoko Ono

Suite at the Ritz
Afternoon tea
Soft lighting
Casual in jeans
Signature shades
Looking intently through them
Finding her eyes
Windows to the soul
Glazed over
Mist of memories
John
Intimate sharing
Opening for a stranger
Remarkable really
Won over so warmly
By woman
Who broke up the Beatles
Fans not seeing
A great love story
Such violent and horrific loss
Talk of music and art
The avant-garde
He as an artist
Their work together
The purpose of the visit
Exhibition of his work
Clap of her hands
Assistant appeared from other room
Took our picture
She snuggling
Me squirming on the couch

Shirt collar
Sticking up akimbo
Brief moment
In the history of time

Afternoon tea with Yoko at the Ritz. Charles Giuliano photo © 2015.

Lizard King

Cold February morning
Père Lachaise Cemetery
Asked officials
Oú est le tombe de Jim Morrison
Pointing
Là à droite
Rude brusque answer
Pourquois
Soon knew why
On tombstones
Jim and arrows
Bronze bust long since gone
Died in a bathtub
Adonis
Past prime
Grave hemmed in
Cramped
Graffiti everywhere
Flowers and poems
Steady flow of visitors
Rock pilgrims
Riders of the storm
Playing guitars
Drinking smoking
Me taking pictures
Eventually an installation
Pimpled punk objected
In rough French
Slurred
Jim belongs to the youth of the world
You are old and fat

Moi cussed back
I was at Woodstock
Where were you
Milk sucking sot
Another kid said
Wow man really
Shoved the punk
Left screaming
Stoned by noon
Paris blues

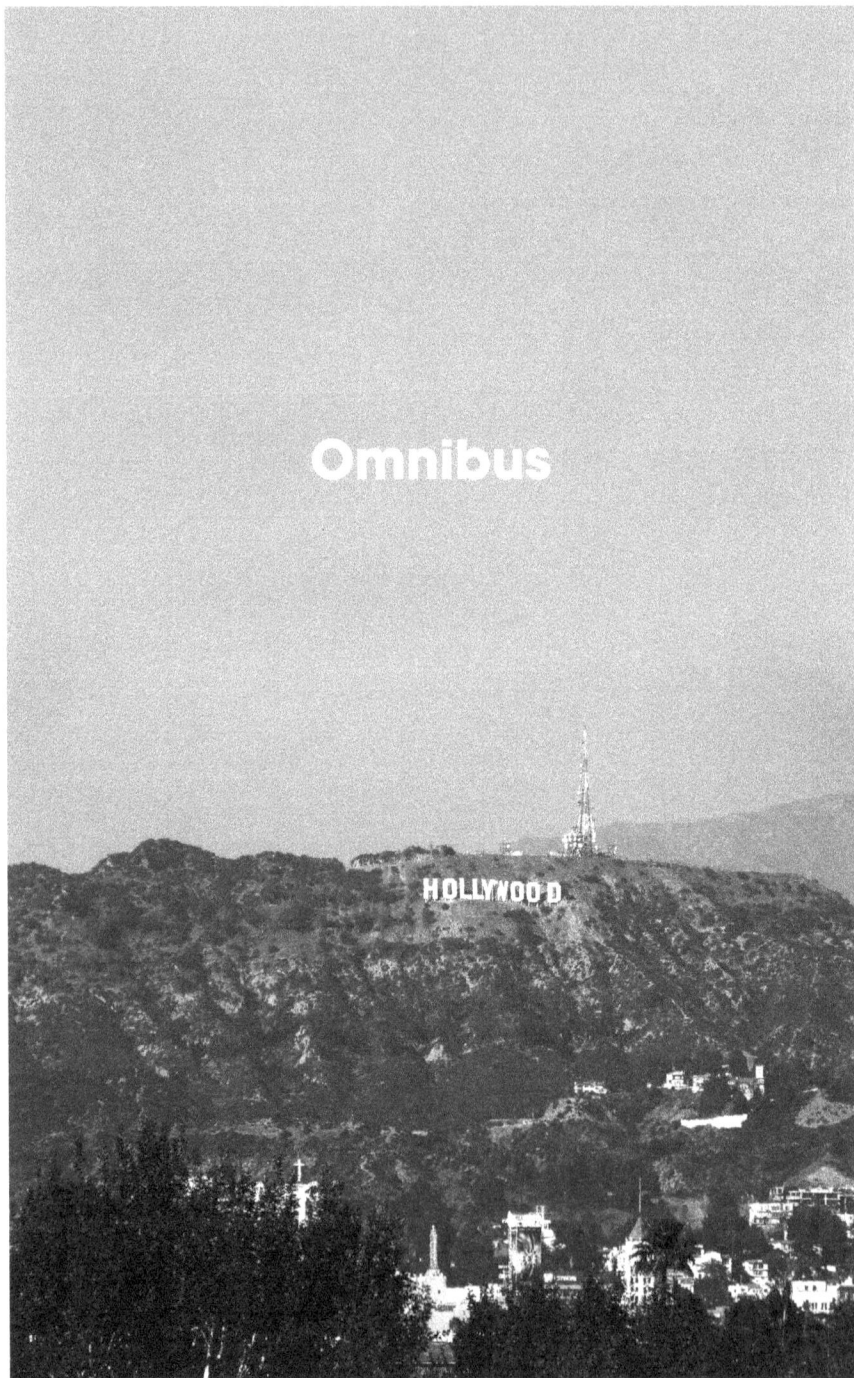

Omnibus

Hollywood sign from the LA County Museum of Art.

Sed Festival

Jubilee Year
Fifty years of rule
Pharaoh rose from the throne
Disrobed
Loincloth and sandals
Double crown
Entrusted to vizier
Ruler of two worlds
Upper and Lower Egypt
Dynasty One
The court circled the track
Started running
At first briskly
The living god
Horus on earth
Slowed by age
Staggered and fell
Dispatched by warriors
Ninety days later
Embalmed
Entombed with treasures
Food for eternal journey
Joined Osiris
The young King
Buried his father
Began
Preparing his funeral

Bear

Basement office
View of backyard
Stranger looking in
Large glass door
Bear cub
Fleeting rare encounter
Grabbing a camera
Already plodding off
As they do
The other day
Sleek fox
Honey colored fur
Now and then turkeys and deer
Friggin pesty groundhogs
Eating flowers
Wasted our herbs
Lives under the lower deck
Multiplies seasonally
Reflections of a
Country gentleman
Wandering the heath with
Shotgun and hound
Berkshire living

A bear cub visiting the studio.

Elevated Interaction

Gallery openings
Rushing around 57th Street
Tuesday nights
List clipped from Sunday Times
Decades ago
Eccentric artist friend
Spotted Harold Rosenberg
After Clement Greenberg
Second most influential critic
Handed his card
Mr. Rosenberg
I'm Raeford Liles
A very fine artist
Would be pleased to have you
Visit my studio
Cramped loft near
Port Authority
Markets for
Gourmet meals
Cooked on a hot plate
Gazing down
Very tall and imposing
I no longer do studio visits
We got off
Unfazed
Doesn't hurt to ask Charlie
Lesson learned
Don't hit on critics
In elevators

Skills

The Big Apple
Many New Yorkers
Don't drive
Can't swim
But have unique skills
Hailing cabs in the rain
A blood sport
Making reservations
Visiting museums
Crashing parties
Scoring theater tickets
Buying wholesale
Shopping at Zabar's
Getting out of town
Rooting for the
Damn Yankees

No Encores

Never stayed for encores
Covering rock concerts
Back in the day
Dragging a date down the aisle
First to leave the parking lot
Race to the office
Composing a lead in my head
In the car
Midnight deadline
Scribbled notes
Mostly song titles
One take
Five hundred words
Out to the City Desk
Editors around the rim
Dropped down the shoot
Hot type below
Chinatown
Mailbag edition
Dropped at the newsstand
Fresh type
Dense ink words raised
Braille
So Zen
First thoughts best thoughts
Like this

Mad As Hell

Charley Don't Surf

Smell of napalm in the morning

Absurdity

Fog of war

Not some Asian village

Forget about

Up the river for Kurtz

The Horror The Horror

Not there

No Lt. William H. Calley, Jr.

My Lai Massacre

This time

Blue team

Justice not just blind

Deaf and dumb

Our own backyard

Brother against brothers

Burn baby burn

Global racism

Home to roost

iPhone

Superduper iPhone
Not yet released
Review copy
Tons of apps
Direct line to God
Called
This is Heaven how may I direct your call
I want to speak to God
Can you hold please
Music Gustav Holst The Planets
Please be patient
All of our operators are busy with other calls
This is Jennifer
Your call may be recorded and monitored
For training purposes
What is your credit card number, expiration date
Can I speak to God
What does this pertain to
Creation
He's busy
Can He get back to you
Not really
This can't wait
Would you like to speak with Jesus
He may be available
Nope I need to speak to the boss
That may not be possible sir
He's really busy
We hope you understand
Have you tried the Pope
People seem to like him

No I need to speak to God
Immediately
Sir please be patient
When is a good time to call
Sundays before 7 AM local time
Usually he's resting
Now and then he likes to chat
Thanks for the call
We appreciate your business

Thanksgiving 2014

White Christmas
Bait and switch
Actually Thanksgiving
Woke to
Fourteen inches in the Berkshires
Currier and Ives
View of Mt. Greylock
Branches bending
Across backyard meadow
Turkey day
Schoolboy games buried under
Slopes open
Early ski season
Climate change
Can't be denied
Dead of winter
Way too soon

Bang

Sure
He separated night from day
Created the earth and moon
Got the kids started
All the creatures
Then rested
Not for seven days
More like seven billion years
On some Club Med galaxy
Playing cosmic golf
Got lonely
Then
By the way
Almost an afterthought
Showed up
Gave Moses the tablets
Creating right and wrong
Thousands of years of wars
In His name
Long after we bleep out
Billions of years from now
Lights out
Bang turned to whimper

Tug of War

Ferguson
The day after
White killer cop
Gets off
Cruise ship America
Multiple decks
Stacked melting pot
Boiling over
Ship of state
Harbor of public opinion
Dead in the water
Nudged to the dock of consensus
Tugged and pushed
Small powerful
Engines
Political forces
Turning us into the headwind
Of change

Moosh Magique

Dead of winter
Acid night in the Berkshires
Holiday gathering
Orgy in the attic
Changed lives
By the hearth
Moosh Magique
Dancing in the flames
Melting mandalas
Oracles of color
Toward dawn
Wrote a check
Fifty years and no sense
Burned it
Ashes to ashes
Went outside
Cold crisp morning early light
Dog barking in the distance
Seeing for miles and miles and miles

Famous Florida-Mountain Turnip

Just around the bend
Jaeschke's Apple Orchard
Thanksgiving this week
Went by for
Famous
Florida-Mountain Turnip
And apples
Small pears
Seckel I asked
No Asian
Got some Seckels though
In the cooler
Just one tree
Not much yield this year
Bought them all
Five pounds
Real sweet
Gave one to the Mexican
He said
Smiled
Muy bueno
Kid growing up
Neighbors had a tree
Snuck in and stole some
Got any cut-up turnip
Need a chain saw
Big project
Keep asking the boss for some
Maybe over the weekend
Got a thousand pounds
In the cooler

Sold a hundred pounds yesterday

What's your number

Call came

Bought five pounds cubed

Twice the price

Worth it

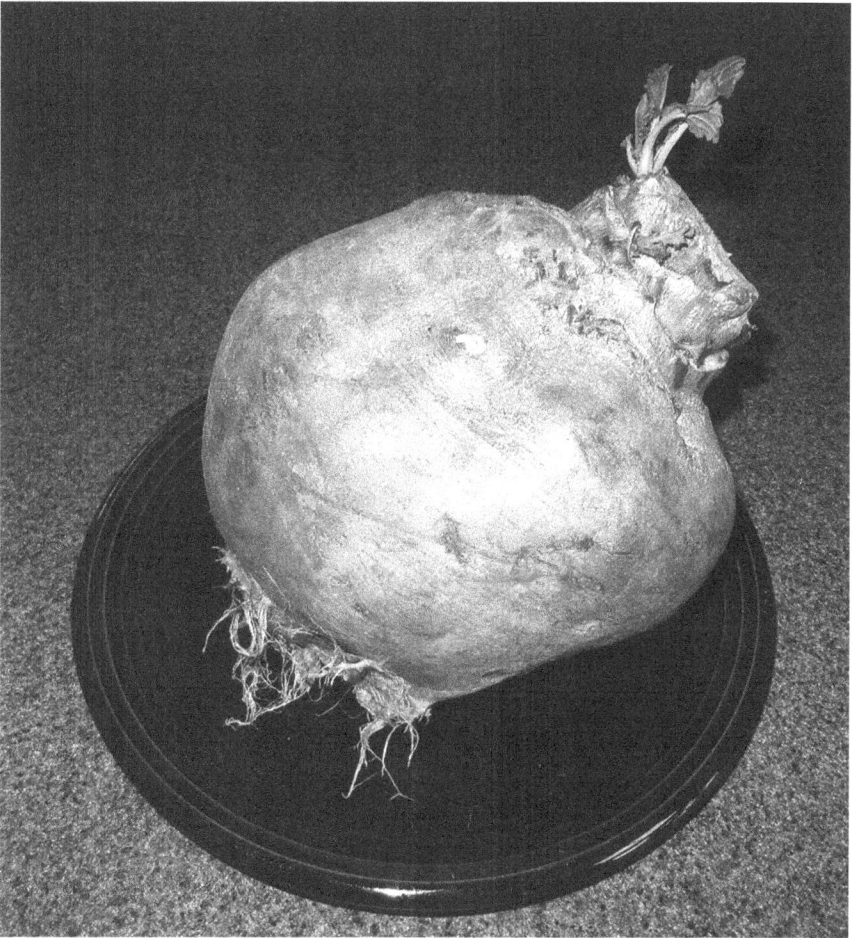

The famous Florida-Mountain Turnip.

Vintage

Christmas Eve
Mount Shango
Festive dinner
Two bottles of 1940s
French wine
War years
Super rare
Part of an art deal
Carefully opened
Gently decanted
Sediment avoided
Sip on the lips
Initial taste
Rested for twenty minutes
Poured
Consumed as it blossomed
Explosion of flavors
Peaked
Then died
Aftertaste of
The fallen

Irish Sports Pages

Calling Mom in Palm Beach

Some years ago

Remember Mrs. so and so

She died

Remember Mr. so and so

Assisted living

Checking the Irish Sports Pages

No mention of me yet

Still among the living

At least for now

Remembered for a moment

Then gone

Forever and ever

Not preserved

Like mummified pharaohs

Just poof

Until then

Living it up

Big time

Silence

Take a number
Sit down and shut up
Wait till we call you
That never happens
Delving into a new field
Insiders have lots of advice
How to do it better
Like them
Thanks but no dice
The arts
Endless turf wars
Ruthless rejection
As my mentor Ian Forman said
Back in the early days
Charlie
In this business
You have to have elephant hide

Calendar

Solstice

For me

Not December 21 for winter

Or June 21 for summer

Not when

Rising sun splits Stonehenge

Or slices into the chamber of Newgrange

But marked by socks

On for winter

Recently on November 2

Cold feet

Or off for the season

Some time in April

Body

Most reliable

Clock and calendar

Movie Stars

In LA
Even
Movie stars
Get stuck
Bumper to bumper
On expressways

Stranger Than

Dinner with friends

Talked about her book group

Saul Bellow

Do you read

Hannah Arendt

Slowly

Fiction

Not much

Why

They make things up

Wright Stuff

From local materials
Stone and cement
Students and fellows
Learned and labored
Arizona desert
Winter quarters school and studios
Taliesin West
Wide-open space
Clear distant mountains
Indian land long abandoned
Low structures embracing nature
Annual caravan migrations
From Wisconsin
Shock on arrival
Power lines marring prized panorama
Called Truman
Take it down
No such luck
Pack everything we leave tomorrow
For Tucson
Third wife made sense
Then mid-eighties
Late to start over
Wright
Redesigned the view
Now signal towers
Top that distant peak
Nada
Today pristine

A view of Taliesen West by Wright.

Volcano

Up the steep slope
Challenging ascent
Billowing sulfurous smoke
Hands and knees
Inching forward
The edge
Red rimmed
Belching ash
Choking and gasping
With a surge
Over the top
Eyeballs cooking
We gazed
Deep in its bowels
Lava bubbling
Bat-winged prince
Tearing melting flesh
Howling soul writhing
Harrowing glimpse
Branded in memory
Scrambled ascent
Years later
Lunch
Crisp Chardonnay
Tall slim glasses
Clinked
Toast
To the Volcano
Recalling youth
What Volcano
You know

The volcano

Don't know what you're talking about

How can you say that

You were there

Beside me

Staring into the ass of hell

Man that was something

Never happened

Besides

A long time ago

Who can remember

You confuse me

With somebody else

Never had this conversation

Get over it

That volcano was never real

For me it was

Still feel the heat

Monster

Tearing at my flesh

Seems like

Yesterday

Critic

Spotted in Harvard Square
You're that critic
Hostile confrontation
You spent ten minutes at my show
Al Ford's gallery off Atlantic Avenue
Trashed it
Oh yes I recalled
Describing every painting
Mostly vertical
Pubescent girls on bikes
Huge sensual innocent eyes
Perky breasts
Cartoonish
Glowing Globe article
Former computer programmer
Morphed as artist
Actually
Spent too much time
Back then looking
Proto post modern
Today probably
Whitney Biennial
Like Lisa Yuskavage
Or John Currin
Who knew
Just a few moments
Lasting impressions
Decades later
Still see that show

Too vividly
Now writing about it
Every artist should get
Such bad reviews

Sketch of Charles Giuliano the critic by the artist Henry Schwartz.

Octopus

Octopus
Dried out lying on the ground
Lifeless
Poked at it curiously
Turned it over
Suddenly
Ferociously grabbed my hand
Wrapped its tentacles
Squeezing
Terrible shooting pains
Venomous stinging sensation
Shook furiously
Trying to break loose
Tugging
With my other hand
It was so strong
Flinging it to the ground
Finding a rock
Pounding it to a pulp
Why are you trying to kill me
It screamed
You said you would be my friend
Please
I won't do it again
Trust me
Just let me be
Reminded of a pledge
Vaguely remembered
Quandary
Not quite sure
Wanting

Such a clinging venomous
Companion
Sobbing and pleading
Now wretched
Walked away
Saddened to abandon
However strange
A loved one

Sicilian Valhalla

Not
Ship set ablaze at sea
Noble warrior
Viking funeral
Rather
In floppy hat
Vampire teeth fashioned from orange peel
Grandfather
Chasing a child
Playing amid tomato plants
Harvest time
Grabbing his chest
Gasping in pain
Shortness of breath
The boy frightened
Running for help
Discovered
Amid the vines
Glorious demise
Death of the Don
Sicilian Valhalla

Di-no-mite

Dreadnoughtus

Or fears nothing

Roamed what is now

Argentina

Some 7 million years ago

Give or take a mill

Why quibble

Weighed in at 65 tons

That's 15 tons more than a Boeing 737

Vegetarian

What an appetite

Weaponized tail

At thirty feet quite a swing

Whacking you upside the head

Long gone

Like us one day

Not far from now

At the rate we're going

Just smarter dinosaurs

Perhaps not really

Where was God

Way back then

Just hanging loose

Till we showed up

To die for

Hartley

German Military Series
Officer Lover killed
WWI
Returned to NY
Stieglitz couldn't sell them
Paint America
With O'Keefe in New Mexico
Gloucester's Dogtown Common
Vinalhaven Maine
Cavorted with fishermen
Giant brothers
Toilers of the deep
Hartley finally happy
They drowned

Nature

Lee Krasner arranged it

Studio visit

Hans Hofmann

Mentor to Post War artists

Looking about

Paused then turned

Reflecting

You should work from nature

Pollock replied sharply

I am nature

Native Dancer

The G, Barry and Me
Hit the Zone
Afternoon Gentleman's Club
On the bar
Bent over backwards
Working girl
Snatch shot
Nursing over-priced drinks
Reaching over
Whipped off Savenor's Prince Valiant
Blond wig
Scruffy balding head
Fell on her ass
Laughing

Barry Savenor without the Prince Valiant wig.

Recap

Winter
Is when you lose stuff
Hats and gloves
Stuffed in jacket pockets
Back in the 1960s
Uncle Freddy
A true eccentric
Sported a beret
Worn then only if you were
French, gay or an artist
I have several
Broad one from Basque country
Too treasured to risk
Bought an NFL wool cap
For a buck
Not Pats
Wrong logo
Philadelphia Eagles
Ragged about it
New York bullies
Your team sucks
Probably
How would I know
Still upset when it went missing
After several winning seasons
Whipping it out
Warm and snug against the cold
Need mittens on a string
Like when I was a kid
Today New Year's
On the way to the gym

Astrid found it

Crushed down in the back seat

Damn you screwed up my poem

Write a new ending

Cap and me

Lost and found

Roadkill

Truck flipped
Driver killed
News today
Last April
Coming out of Arkansas
Traffic crawl
Two hours passing wreck
Driving rain
Headed east
Stop and go
White knuckles
Eight-hour days
Listening to jazz
Chatting
Rear-view mirror
Truck closing in fast
Hit the accelerator
Surged ahead
Behind
Swerved off then back on
Big rig exited
Close call
Vacation
Could have ended in
Roadkill

Cedar Tavern

Spring break the 1960s

Art student in New York

Headed to the Cedar Tavern

82 University Place between 11th and 12th Street

Mecca for artists

Legendary stories

Arguments and brawls

Pollock drunk lifting skirts

De Kooning in a booth

Studio secrets revealed

A weeknight

Nobody around

Ordered a beer

Sipped slowly

Nothing happened

Just another bar

No insights

Still looking

Séance

Garden apartment
303 East 11th street
Lower East Side
Living on the dole
Steamy summer
No utilities
Candles at night
Window wide
Cat jumped in
Threw it out
Jumped in
Threw it out
Relented
Bought food and litter
OK pal let's tough it out
Mooshie Cat
Sat on my chest purred
Gently dug in claws
Hours licking mangled fur
Started to shine
Uptown for a séance
Sybil Leek's American coven
Is there a spirit in the room
Table tapping
Back home Mooshie sick
Nursed all night
Phone booth calls to Animal Rescue
Headed there
Bundled up on a bus
Croaked in my arms
Walking home at dawn

Ironic bright sun

Passing trash cans

Couldn't do it

Put Mooshie in a paper bag

Stuffed in the freezer

Down and out

Jim took me to the Berkshires

Stayed in the Church

Bell tower

Rang it in the morning

Winter then Spring

Landlord provided old doors

Gerry and I enclosed the yard

Cleaned up the trash

Ground finally soft

Mooshie buried

Medium with a message

Dissent

J'Accuse
Émile Zola 1898
Alfred Dreyfus Affair
French anti-Semitism
Analyzed by Hannah Arendt
Slow reading
Origins of Totalitarianism
Brandeis undergraduate 1960s
Contentious debates
Eichmann trial in Jerusalem
Arendt's controversial New Yorker coverage
Radical campus
Abbie Hoffman, Herbert Marcuse, Angela Davis
Coffee with Angela in the snack bar
Friend of Evan Stark
Flunked Chemistry
Lab partner blew up a bank
Importance of dissent
Radical generation
Joan Baez singing in a dormitory
Trips to Club 47 in Cambridge
Rachel Goldstein loved her
My car
Spring break with Mel Lyman in Harlan County
Acid trip night before graduation
Not exactly kosher
Outrageous

Anthems of another time
Still not free
Mushroom clouds
Explode within

Jules Olitski

Alfa Romeo
Sleek and beautiful
Like Italians
Temperamental
Bought with mad money
Sales from first exhibition
That summer 1960s
Driving around
Signing artists to make prints
United Church of Christ
Portfolio
In Vermont
Meeting Jules Olitski
Brief encounter
Minutes really after
Hours of driving
Car overheated
Had to return asking for water
Visitor arrived
Warm greetings
Jules and Clem
Years later
Shows at the MFA
Interview for Boston After Dark
Shades drawn
Suite at the Ritz
Ordering room service
What will you have
Coffee for me
Jules asked for
Johnny Walker Black Label

Water glasses full
Downed as we talked
Paris on the GI Bill
Living on peanuts and coffee
Opening that night
More Scotch
From utter poverty to fame
Pain drowned
What price
Glory

Dante on the Elevator

Between Heaven and Hell
Were Dante alive today
He would say
Ride the elevator
Heaven and Hell
Night and day
Spiritual chiaroscuro
Virgil the operator
Changed at purgatory
Pagan denied salvation
Descending levels
Gothic circles
Sinners
Feeling the heat
Sweating it out
Bottoming with betrayers
Damned and wretched
Booted out by Charon
The eternal ennui
Boredom of Sartre's
Other People
Penance
Rising up through the
Flagellants
Backs whipped raw
Grim Goya painting
Rising through Purgatory
The nowhere land
Neither damned nor saved
Eternal apathy
Suspended animation

2

Unending hibernation
Burst through the clouds
Paradiso
Martyrs and saints
Souls of the saved
Disembodied angels
Sexless smiling faces
Oozing goodness and grace
Like Iowa in summer
No place for hipsters

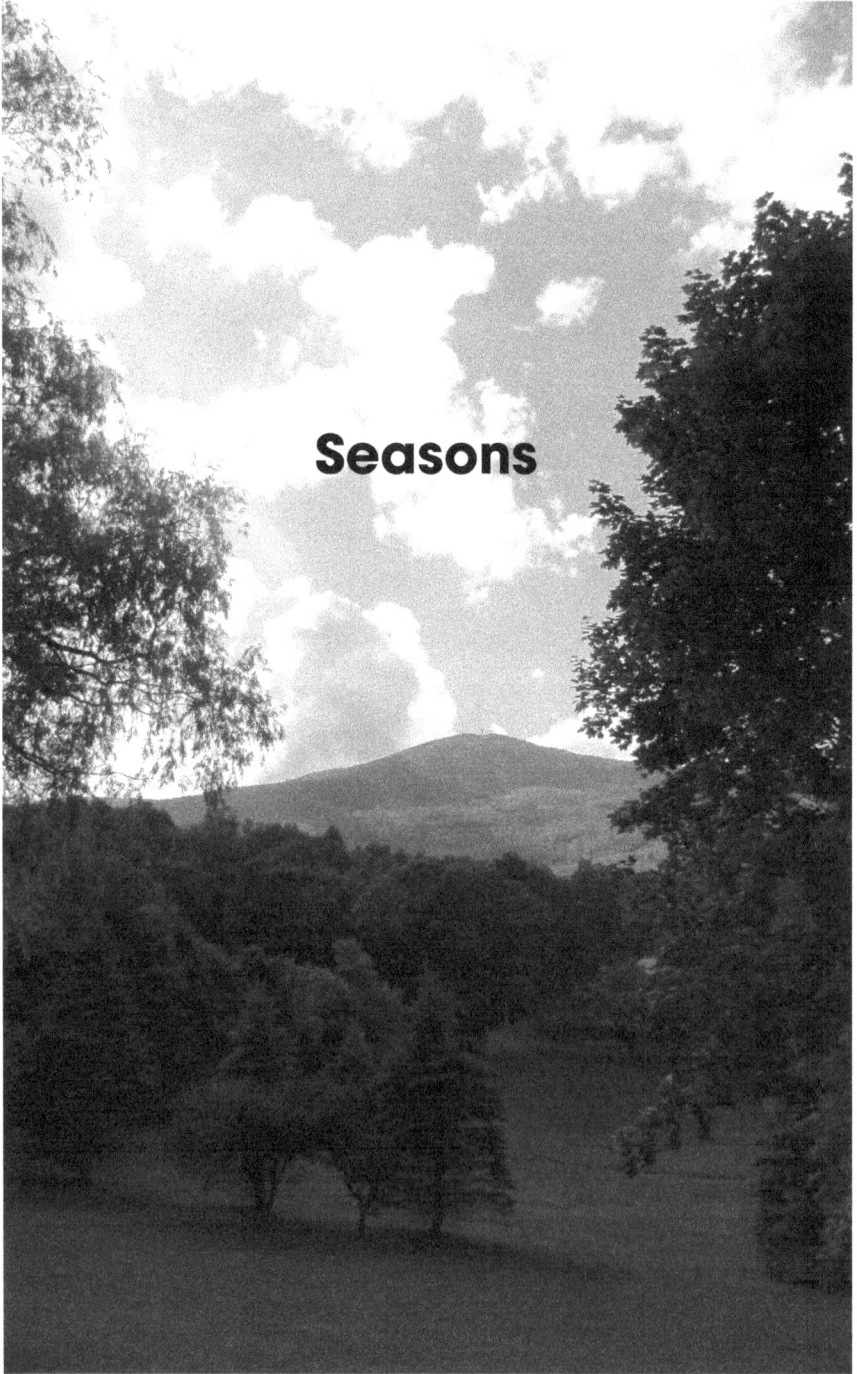

Seasons

The ever-changing view of Mt Greylock from our backyard.

Magic Mountain

Backyard view
Across several acres
Original farmhouse
Beyond it Mt. Greylock
Highest peak in Massachusetts
Some 3,491 feet
Tower and Bascomb Lodge at the summit
Our clock and calendar
Ever-changing movie
First light to dusk
Constant primordial
Always incrementally different
From frosted to verdant
Lush or bare
Richly painted in fall
Gray and bristled winters
Like Joseph's
Coat of many colors
Woven by nature
Worn on
Broad back of unbending time

January

Hunkered down
Projects
Catching up
Contemplating
Recouping from months of travel
Slower pace
Short cold days
Janus
Two faced Roman god
Looking forward and back
Counting
Revolutions of earth around the sun
Since when and for how long
Year, month, day, hour, minute, second
Humanistic measures
All relative
What time is it
In the Milky Way
Compared to what
Out there
Deep space
The beyond
In now 2015
What does that mean

Winter Birches Magic. Astrid Hiemer photo © 2015.

December

Vrooooom
The fastest month of the year
So much to do, so little time
Ho, ho, ho
All that cheer
Utterly exhausting
Jingle Bells blasting away
From Big Y to Walmart
Sell, sell, sell
Buy, buy, buy
Frenzied acquisitions
Latest kitchen gadgets
Years of pearls and jewelry
Irish sweaters
Exotic perfumes and emollients
Long gone
Winter wonderland
For a time playful and fun
Not so white-knuckling to the airport
Picking up Astrid
Nearest hotel for a
Honeymoon
Home from DC and the grandchildren
Me busted knee from a week in NY
Rockefeller Center and all that
Broadway and museums
Slogging about
Broken elevator at The Club
Second oldest in the city after
The Morgan Library
Bags hauled up and down three flights

Limping through the holidays
And to all a good night
More like
Good grief
Advil in the eggnog

Deep in the woods.

November

Day after Halloween
Christmas shopping
Blustery return to the Berkshires
Three weeks
Phoenix and LA
Summer we never had
Hunkered down
Winter coming
Red Tide
Dismal morning after elections
Pays to advertise
America's hearts and minds
For sale
Obama bashing
Lame duck
More D.C. gridlock
Planet
Going to hell
Holidays
Bah humbug

Backyard Adams wild turkeys evoke the holidays.

October

Mr. October
Hero with a bat
Last year glorious
Red Sox won it all
This season
Dead last
Total bust
No Joy in Mudville
Harvesting
Abundance of herbs
Pesto for the freezer
Meager crop of tomatoes
Each a delicious gift
More like dessert
Enjoyed last night
David and Ellen
Her birthday
He helped me to plant
Former Kibbutznik
Love of soil
Thoughts of coming winter
Sharing plans
Projects with Astrid in the loft
Until then
Yard work
Hunkering down
Too soon
Frost on the pumpkin
On the 25th
Birthday

Shared with Picasso and Jonas Salk

Françoise Gilot

Bedded them both

But not me

September Song

Eons

Astrid grew these sunflowers.

September

Billions of years then to now
Calibrated to the birth of Christ
Celestial rotations
Earth a speck of sand in the beach of space
A time of harvest
Food from local farms
Until frost
Last of the sweet corn
Cool wet summer
Followed a brutal winter
Global warming
Severe weather events
Rising oceans laced with mercury
Past the tipping point
From Venus of Willendorf to Selfies
Some 30,000 years more or less
Nest now fouled
Half life countdown
Just a matter of time
How many more generations
Filled with greed and hate
Constantly at war home and abroad
Harvest again
Feeding seven billion

August

Roman calendar
Named for Augustus
Born Gaius Octavius
Crops maturing
Herbs in abundance
Tomatoes again disappointing
Too cool and rainy
Invasives choking trees
Skeletons held up by vines
Environment gone rogue
Pythons in the Everglades
Ravaged planet
Of billions of years
Wasted by man in just 30,000
Extinction inevitable
Stalled by
Better gadgets and technology
Eventually
Rachel Carson's Silent Spring
Not if but when

www.ingramcontent.com/pod-product-compliance
Lightning Source LLC
LaVergne TN
LVHW011230080426
835509LV00005B/425